ADAPTED FOR SUCCESS

LIONS

AND OTHER MAMMALS

Andrew Solway

Heinemann Library
Chicago, Illinois

CL

Customer Service   888–454–2279

Visit our website at www.heinemannlibrary.com

Photo research by Mica Brancic and Susi Paz
Designed by Richard Parker
Printed and bound in China by WKT Company Ltd

11 10 09 08 07
10 9 8 7 6 5 4 3 2 1

Library of Congress Cataloging-in-Publication Data
Solway, Andrew.
  Lions and other mammals / Andrew Solway.
     p. cm. -- (Adapted for success)
  Includes bibliographical references and index.
  ISBN-13: 978-1-4034-8220-4 (library binding (hardcover))
  ISBN-10: 1-4034-8220-9
  ISBN-13: 978-1-4034-8227-3 (pbk.)
  ISBN-10: 1-4034-8227-6
  1. Lions--Juvenile literature. 2. Mammals--Juvenile literature. I. Title. II. Series: Solway, Andrew. Adapted for success.
  QL737.C23S583 2006
  599.757--dc22
                            2006014289

Acknowledgments
The author and publisher are grateful to the following for permission to reproduce copyright material:
Corbis pp. 4 (right), 16, pp. 7 (Gallo Images/Martin Harvey), 29 (Gallo Images/Nigel J. Dennis), 38 (Joel W. Rogers), 14 (Kevin Schafer), 28, 32 (Momatiuk – Eastcott), 6 (Niall Benvie), 9 (Rob Howard), 11 (Terry W. Eggers), 19 (Tom Brakefield), 39 (Sygma/Bagla Pallava); Getty pp. 43 (AFP), 21 (Digital Vision), 36 (Gallo Images), 4 (left), 4 (middle), 5, 8, 11, 42 (PhotoDisc), 26–27, 35 (National Geographic), 18 (Photonica), 22 (Stock Image), 24 (Getty Stone), 23 (Taxi), 20, 40 (The Image Bank), 37 (Visuals Unlimited); NHPA pp. 41 (ANT Photo Library), 34 (Jonathan & Angela Scott); Science Photo Library pp. 10 (Peter Chadwick), 12 (Tom McHugh).

Cover photograph of snarling lion with ears back reproduced with permission of Alamy/ © Steve Bloom Images.

The publishers would like to thank Ann Fullick for her assistance in the preparation of this book.

Contents

Some words are shown in bold, **like this**. You can find out what they mean by looking in the glossary.

Descended from Shrews

Lions are among the most awesome **predators** in the world. They belong to a group of animals known as **mammals**. These are **warm-blooded**, usually furry animals that feed their young milk. There is a huge variety of different mammals—polar bears in the Arctic, camels in the desert, whales in the ocean, and bats in the air. All these different mammals are descended from small insect-eating animals that lived many millions of years ago.

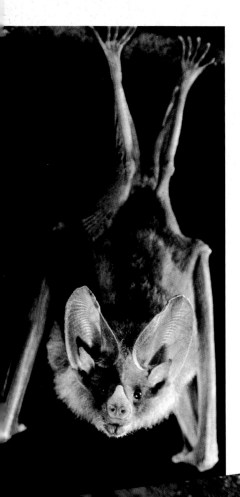

Small insect-eaters

The earliest mammals appeared about 200 million years ago. They were small creatures that lived in trees and looked like modern shrews. At about the same time, the first dinosaurs appeared. The dinosaurs quickly became the dominant type of animal on land, while mammals remained small and fewer in number.

Then about 65 million years ago, something happened that caused all the dinosaurs to become **extinct**. Many scientists think that the main cause was a huge **meteorite** (rock from space) that hit Earth and caused great destruction.

The dinosaurs died out, but mammals survived. They began to spread and fill many of the **habitats** that had been dominated by dinosaurs for so many years. The mammals **adapted** in order to survive in these new habitats. As the mammals changed, they became different from each other, and many new **species** of mammals arose.

What is a success?

What does it mean for a species or group of animals to be successful? There are several ways you could measure the success of a group of animals. One way might be to count the number of individuals of a species or the number of species within a group. However, numbers are not really a good measure of success. A habitat can support many more small animals than large ones, and also a larger variety of smaller species.

Another measure of success might be the **range** of a species. An animal such as a fox or a badger, which has adapted to live in many habitats worldwide, is perhaps more successful than an animal that can live only in one habitat. This is a better measure of success because it shows how adaptable a species is.

A third measure of success could be the length of time that a species or group has survived. By this measure, mammals are more successful than dinosaurs because they have survived for 200 million years. Dinosaurs died out after about 150 million years.

Mammals are adapted to live in many different ways. Many bats live mainly in the air. Foxes are among the most wide-ranging of all mammals. Polar bears live in the Arctic, while lions are adapted to grassy plains.

How Does Adaptation Work?

Evolution is the process by which life on Earth has developed and changed. Life first appeared on Earth 3.5 billion years ago. Since then, living things have evolved from simple single **cells** to the estimated 10 million or more different species on Earth today.

Squirrels are rodents. Like other rodents they have two large teeth for eating nuts and other tough plant material.

Useful changes

Adaptation is an important part of evolution. Adaptations are ways in which a living thing changes to fit into a particular environment and way of life. A bat's wings, for instance, are adaptations for flying. The teeth of a **carnivore** are adapted for slicing through meat, while those of a **herbivore** are adapted to grind up plants. How, then, does adaptation happen?

Variation

Not all individuals of the same species are exactly the same. You can see this yourself if you look at the people in your class at school. Some people are taller than others. Some people have light hair, while others have dark hair. Some people are musical, and some are good at sports. These differences among individuals of a species are known as **variations**.

Natural selection

The variation among individuals makes it possible for a species to adapt. The driving force for adaptation is called **natural selection**. Animals **compete** with each other for food, space, and safe places to bring up their young. Individuals of the same species also compete with each other for **mates**. The animals that are best adapted to their environment survive to **reproduce** and pass on their helpful characteristics to their **offspring**.

If there are changes in the environment where a species lives, natural selection will favor those individuals that help the species adapt. About 18 million years ago, horses, which until then had lived in forests, moved on to grassland. In open grass-lands, a key to surviving attacks from predators is to be a fast runner. Horses as a species quickly adapted to become fast runners. They grew bigger, their legs grew longer, and they began to stand permanently on tiptoe.

ALL IN THE GENES

Living things pass on characteristics to their offspring through their **genes**. A living thing's genetic material is a kind of instruction book for that individual.

Most animals and plants produce offspring by sexual reproduction. Males and females each produce special cells, known as **gametes**, which have only half the normal genetic material. Each parent provides half the genetic information for its offspring.

In the breeding season males compete with each other to get mates. Male kangaroos have boxing matches to decide who will mate with a female.

Where Lions Live

Mammals have adapted to live in all kinds of habitat. Yaks live in high mountains, prairie dogs live in underground burrows, dolphins swim in the ocean, and bats fly through the air.

Lions have adapted to live in open woodlands, grassy plains, **savannah**, and semi-desert. Unlike tigers and leopards, they are not adapted to living in thick forest.

Lions usually live in grassland or savannah, such as this savannah in Kenya.

Changing habitats

Today few lions survive outside game reserves and other protected areas. Most lions live in Africa, south of the Sahara desert, although a small group lives in the Gir Forest nature reserve in India. In these areas there are plenty of large **prey** animals such as antelopes, zebras, and wildebeest for the lions to eat.

From about 1.6 million years ago until as recently as 10,000 years ago, lions lived in many more areas than today. They were found across the world, from southern Europe to the east of India, and in large areas of North America. The exact reasons why their range has shrunk so much are not clear. Changes in climate meant that thick forests covered much of Europe. This was not a good habitat for lions. Humans also had an effect. They hunted both the lions themselves and the lions' prey. Lions disappeared from North America about 10,000 years ago, from Europe about 2,000 years ago, and from the Middle East during medieval times (about 700 years ago).

Grassland adaptations

Lions are best adapted to grassland and savannah environments. Their sandy coat is the color of dead grass and blends in well with the grassland. They have keen eyesight and hearing, which are excellent for finding prey in the open spaces of grassland and savannah.

A lion's roar is an important adaptation to life in open habitats. In open country a lion's roar can be heard five miles (eight kilometers) away. Lions live in loose social groups called **prides**. Lions within a pride can recognize the roars of other pride members. Roaring helps them keep in touch with each other. Male lions also roar to warn other males to stay away from their **territory**.

THE TSAVO LIONS

Lions from the Tsavo area in Kenya show several differences from other lions, which experts think are adaptations to their environment. The Tsavo wildlife reserve is hot and dry and full of thick thorn bushes. In this environment a heavy mane is a real disadvantage. Most male Tsavo lions do not have a mane. The main prey animals of Tsavo lions are water buffalo, which can weigh 2,200 pounds (1,000 kilograms). Tsavo lions are often bigger than other lions, which is probably an adaptation to catching very large prey.

This photo of a male Tsavo lion shows the reduced mane.

Mammals in Different Environments

In the same way that lions are adapted to grassland life, other mammals are adapted to survive in a wide variety of different environments. Some mammals have changed physically. Other mammals look similar but have adapted in other ways.

Big physical changes

Whales and dolphins are so well adapted to life in water that they look more like fish than mammals. Their bodies have become streamlined to glide easily through the water. They also have lost their covering of hair, and instead have a layer of blubber (fat) under the skin to keep them warm. Their front legs have developed into fins for controlling their direction, while the back legs have disappeared altogether. To move through the water, the whale uses its broad, powerful tail instead of legs.

Smaller changes inside the body

The oryx looks very similar to other kinds of antelope that live in much wetter areas. However, it is adapted to live in some of the hottest, driest places on Earth.

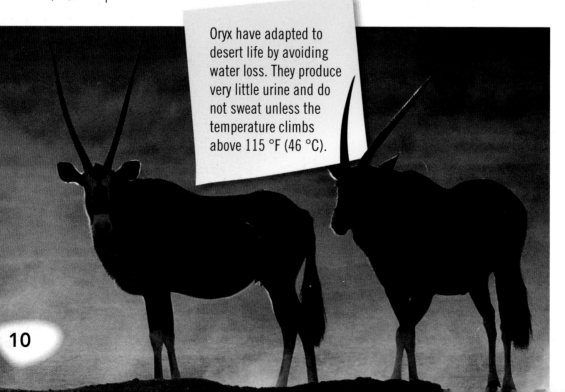

Oryx have adapted to desert life by avoiding water loss. They produce very little urine and do not sweat unless the temperature climbs above 115 °F (46 °C).

For desert animals the key to survival is to avoid losing water. One major way that mammals lose heat in hot climates is by sweating. However, oryx do not sweat. Since they cannot sweat they overheat, but their bodies can tolerate overheating better than other animals.

Another way mammals lose water is through their dung and urine. In an oryx the gut **absorbs** nearly all the water from the dung, which is very dry. The kidneys also are very good at absorbing water, so the oryx produces only a few drops of very concentrated urine.

A jackrabbit (left) and an Arctic hare (right) show the difference in ear size between these two mammals.

Changing behavior

Many mammals adapt to different environments through their behavior. Arabian oryx and gerbils, for instance, look for food in the evening and at night to avoid the worst of the desert heat.

Animals such as foxes, rats, badgers, and raccoons are **generalists** that can survive in a wide range of habitats. These animals can adapt to different foods and can make their dens or nests in a variety of places.

DIFFERENT EARS

With some animals, you can tell where they live by looking at their ears. The Arctic hare, for instance, has small ears compared with other hares of the same size. This is because ears are thin and lose body heat quickly. In the Arctic it is too cold to lose heat this way. On the other hand, jackrabbits in Arizona have enormous ears. Arizona is very hot and the ears keep the rabbits cool by getting rid of excess heat.

Finding a Niche

Within any habitat different mammals live in different areas and in different ways. Each species has its own **niche** (unique place) in the habitat. The niches of different mammals can overlap, but if two animals live in the same niche they will be in **direct competition**. The better-adapted species will get most of the food, and within a short time the species that is less well adapted will die out.

Forest niches

The squirrels that live in the rainforests of western Malaysia show how different species can live in the same habitat but in separate niches. Different species of squirrel live at various levels in the forest. Some live on the ground, some in the middle levels of the forest, and some in the treetops. They also eat different foods—leaves, fruits, insects, or bark and sap. Finally, some squirrel species are active during the day, while others are active at night. Altogether, 25 different species manage to live together in the forest without competing directly.

The red giant flying squirrel lives in southern and eastern Asia. Its habitat is high in the rainforest trees, where it feeds at night on leaves and shoots.

FLYING SQUIRRELS

Many of the squirrels in the Malaysian rainforest have adapted to life in the rainforest canopy by evolving the ability to fly—or, rather, to glide. Flying squirrels have large flaps of skin between their front and back legs. When they want to cross a gap between two trees, they leap and spread their legs wide to stretch out these skin flaps. In this way, flying squirrels can make glides of up to 1,476 feet (450 meters).

Filling empty niches

In any habitat there are millions of different niches, each filled by a different animal. If one species should die out for some reason, other species will compete to take its place. If a whole range of new niches open up, new species will quickly evolve to fill them. This is what happened when the dinosaurs died out. Many of the niches that the dinosaurs had left were filled by mammals, which spread and adapted into many new habitats.

Direct competition

If two species compete directly for the same niche, the species that cannot compete as well will die out. An example of this kind of competition happened about three million years ago, when a bridge of land first formed between North and South America. At the time, most mammals in South America were **marsupials**, like the kangaroos and opossums of Australia today, while all the species in North America were **placental mammals**, like cows, dogs, and humans. Animals spread in both directions, and many species found themselves in direct competition with an animal from the other continent. In most cases the placental mammals were more successful, and the marsupial species died out. For example, jaguars are placental cats that out-competed marsupial sabertooth cats that lived three million years ago.

Top Hunters

A lion's niche in its habitat is as the **top predator**. Other large predators—such as leopards, cheetahs, and spotted hyenas—hunt some of the same animals as lions. However, only lions regularly hunt large prey such as zebra, buffalo, and giraffe.

Lions are well adapted for catching large prey. They can leap on a zebra traveling at high speed, hang on with their claws, and use their great strength to bring it to the ground. Then they kill their prey with a bite to the throat.

Powerful cats

Every part of a lion's body is expertly adapted for hunting. With their agile, flexible bodies, they can creep silently through the grass or leap from the ground suddenly. They have long, pointed **canine teeth** for biting, and a pair of scissor-like **carnassials** at the back of the mouth for slicing through flesh.

Lions have very powerful jaws. With a large animal, such as a zebra, they clamp their jaws around the throat of their prey and suffocate it.

A lion's front legs also are very powerful, for gripping and pulling down prey. It can use its claws to grab victims and to rip open a **carcass**. When the lion is not using its claws, it can retract them into its paws, to keep them razor-sharp.

COOPERATIVE HUNTING

When hunting large prey such as zebras or wildebeest, several lions will often work together as a team. One or more lions will lie in wait, while other lions drive the prey toward them. At the last moment, the waiting lions leap up and attack the prey.

Night hunters

Lions usually hunt in the evening and at night. They have excellent vision in very low light, while the vision of their prey is not as good in the dark. It is also cooler at night, which is better for lions because they do not sweat and must pant like dogs to keep cool. Lions also have excellent hearing, which helps them locate victims while they are hunting in long grass.

Big appetites

Lions need to consume an average of about thirteen pounds (six kilograms) of meat a day. Like other predators, however, they cannot rely on regular meals. At some times prey animals may be plentiful and lions can kill with ease. At other times lions may hunt for many days without catching food.

A lion's big appetite is an adaptation to this hunting way of life. A male lion can eat over 88 pounds (40 kilograms) of meat in one sitting—a week's food in one meal! This helps lions survive periods when prey is scarce.

All Kinds of Food

One way that mammals living in the same habitat avoid direct competition is by eating different foods. The earliest mammals were **insectivores**. However, mammal species have adapted to eat all kinds of food.

Lions are one of many mammal species that are **carnivores**. Mammal carnivores eat all kinds of other animals. For example, hedgehogs and shrews eat insects and worms, lions eat water buffalo, and killer whales eat sea lions.

Ruminants, such as this mountain goat, partly digest their food in the stomach, then bring the food back up into the mouth and chew it a second time.

Eating plants

Many mammals, from mice to elephants, feed on plants. Plant-eaters have different adaptations from carnivores. Plant food is often tough and hard to digest. To help the digestive process, **herbivores** have flat-topped teeth with grooves in them, which grind up the food like millstones grinding wheat.

Plants contain large amounts of a substance called cellulose, which animals cannot digest. Animals that rely entirely on plant food, therefore, have special digestive systems to process their food. **Ruminants** have a series of five stomachs for getting nutrients from their food. Special bacteria in their stomachs help the digestion process by breaking down cellulose.

Other hunters

Not all carnivores are predators. The blue whale, for instance, is a **filter feeder**. This enormous whale, which is the largest creature ever to exist, eats small, shrimp-like creatures called krill. It catches them by sucking up great mouthfuls of seawater containing thousands of krill. Instead of teeth, the blue whale has filters of tough, springy material called baleen. It pushes the seawater out of its mouth through the baleen, which lets out the water but traps the krill.

Omnivores and scavengers

Some mammals are not limited to eating only animals or just plants. Racoons, bears, pigs, foxes, and humans are all **omnivores**—they eat both animal and plant food. Most of the mammals that have adapted best to living around humans are omnivores.

Scavengers are animals that eat dead and rotting meat, or other scraps and waste. Animals such as brown hyenas and Tasmanian devils are specialist scavengers. Their powerful teeth and jaws are strong enough to crack open bones, which other animals cannot do.

SUN FOOD

The food that all mammals eat ultimately comes from the Sun. Plants turn the Sun's energy into food for herbivores, and they, in turn, provide food for carnivores. At each stage in the process energy is lost. This means that a large number of herbivores, and an even larger number of plants, are needed to support one carnivore.

This energy pyramid shows how a habitat can support more plants than herbivores and more herbivores than carnivores.

Unusual Feeding Habits

In any habitat, there is fierce competition for the best food sources. Some animals avoid this competition by feeding on unusual foods that other animals are not adapted to eat.

Sleepy heads

Koalas look like bears, but in fact they are marsupials, more closely related to kangaroos than to bears. They spend most of their lives in eucalyptus trees, eating eucalyptus leaves.

Eucalyptus leaves are tough, full of fibers, and low in nutrition. They also contain poisonous chemicals. However, koalas have adapted to deal with all these problems. A koala's grinding teeth crush the tough leaves into a fine paste. Koalas also avoid leaves with the worst poisons, and their bodies can make other poisons safe. The digestive system includes a long tube called the caecum. Special bacteria in the caecum help break down the eucalyptus leaves.

None of these adaptations changes the fact that eucalyptus leaves are simply not very nourishing. Koalas get through a lot of leaves—up to 2.2 pounds (1 kilogram) every day—but even so, their diet is short on energy. Koalas have adapted to this problem by not doing much! Koalas spend twenty hours of each day asleep, and when they are awake they usually move very slowly. This low-energy lifestyle means that they can survive on a poor diet.

The koala digestive system has adapted to eat the tough, poisonous leaves of eucalyptus (gum trees).

A giant anteater licks up around 35,000 ants and termites each day.

Toothless and sticky-tongued

Another strange source of food is ants. Ants live in large groups, so eating one ant will often cause many other ants to appear and attack the predator. Ants have a painful bite, and they can spray a burning liquid called formic acid if attacked.

Anteaters have adapted to survive on a diet of ants and termites. Their powerful front legs and claws are adapted for breaking open ant and termite nests. They have a long snout for poking into the nests, and a very long, sticky tongue for licking up the ants. To protect themselves from bites, they have rubbery skin and a protective coat of long hairs. They also avoid eating ant species with very painful bites, such as army ants.

Like a diet of eucalyptus leaves, a diet of ants is not rich in energy. Anteaters move slowly so they do not need a lot of energy to live.

YUMMY DUNG

Young koalas live on their mother's milk for about five months. They cannot start eating eucalyptus leaves right away because their caecum does not contain the rich mixture of bacteria that helps adult koalas digest their food and get rid of poisons. To get over this problem, parents produce special nutritious feces (dung) for a short time. The young eat this dung and get the bacteria they need to start their digestion working properly.

19

Disguising an Attack

A lion's sandy coat is the color of dry grass. This makes a lion hard to spot in the grassland and savannah areas where it lives. Lions are top predators, so they do not need **camouflage** to hide from their enemies. However, their coat is adapted to blend in with their surroundings. They use this camouflage to help them creep up on their prey.

A lion crouched motionless in grass can be very difficult to detect.

Stalk and spring

Lions cannot run fast enough to catch fast-moving animals such as antelopes and zebras in a chase. However, they can leap far forward very quickly. From a distance of about 49 feet (15 meters) or closer, they have a good chance of catching their prey. To get this close, they have to stalk their victims.

All cats—from pet cats to lions and tigers—are good at stalking. They can move silently toward their prey, keeping very low to the ground, and using every scrap of cover.

Once the lion is close enough, camouflage becomes unimportant. Over a short distance the lion can move faster than its prey. With small prey, the lion will usually leap on the animal's back and bite into the spinal cord at the back of the neck. For larger animals, the lion will instead try to pull the animal down and bite its throat, hanging on until the victim suffocates.

Spots and stripes

Lions have a plain coat, but many big cats have strong black markings. Cheetahs and leopards, for instance, have spots, while tigers have stripes. These kinds of markings are very good at breaking up the outline of a big cat when it stays still among tall grasses or undergrowth.

Leopards and cheetahs are both powerful predators, but they are no match for a lion or a tiger. Lions and tigers see leopards and cheetahs as rivals, and kill them if they can. Leopards, in particular, are skilled at using their camouflage to hide from other predators.

A DANGEROUS AGE

Newborn lion cubs weigh 100 times less than their mother. They are blind for the first ten days of life, and they cannot walk well before they are one month old. To keep them safe, the mother lion finds a place for her cubs to hide. When the mother is away, the cubs stay still and quiet to avoid being found by predators. Although adult lions have no markings, young lion cubs often have some spotted markings. These spots may help camouflage them.

A leopard's spots are especially good camouflage in forests, where there are patches of light and shade.

Hiding from Each Other

Most mammals use camouflage in some way, either to help them to hide from their enemies or to make it easier to sneak up on their victims. There are several kinds of camouflage. Some mammals have mainly one kind of camouflage, but many have colors and markings that camouflage them in several ways.

Blending in

In some mammals, blending in with their surroundings is very useful. Polar bears and Arctic foxes, for example, both have white coats that are very good at hiding them in their snowy environment. A polar bear lying by a seal breathing hole, waiting for a seal to appear, is almost invisible except for the black patch of its nose. To avoid even this tiny patch showing, polar bears often cover their noses with their paws while they are lying in wait for prey.

Stoats in their white winter coats are known as ermines. Ermines are farmed for their thick, pure white fur.

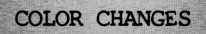

COLOR CHANGES

Many animals living in the Arctic have white or light-colored fur that camouflages them very well. However, some animals do not stay the same color all year long. Mammals such as stoats and Arctic hares are brown in summer for camouflage against the brown earth. When winter comes they shed their brown coat and grow a new, white coat to hide them in the snow.

Special markings

Many kinds of mammals have spots and stripes in their coat. Markings of this kind are known as **disruptive camouflage**. The markings help break up the shape of the animal, which makes it more difficult to recognize. The stripes in a tiger's coat or a leopard's spots are examples of disruptive camouflage.

The strangely marked okapi lives in thick forest, where its mostly dark color blends in well. However, its hindquarters are striped, which is effective at disrupting the okapi's outline. The young of some deer, such as the white-tailed deer of the United States, have spotted disruptive camouflage to help disguise them while they are young and helpless (the adults do not have spots).

The okapi is mostly dark colored to blend in with its forest habitat, but it also has disruptive stripes.

Countershading

Sunlight comes from above, so an animal's body is usually more brightly lit above than it is below. The sunlight creates shadows on the animal's body that call attention to its three-dimensional shape. However, many mammals are more darkly colored above, with a lighter belly area. This **countershading** helps flatten the animal's shape and make it harder to see. Woodland deer, such as chital or fallow deer, have this type of countershading. They also have white spots on their back, which is a kind of disruptive camouflage.

A Zebra's Stripes

The striped coats of zebras stand out in the open grasslands where they live. Zebras and other **grazing** animals wander the plains in large herds rather than living alone and trying to conceal themselves among the grasses. However, the zebra's coat and living in herds are both adaptations that are possibly kinds of camouflage.

Black and white camouflage

To humans, a zebra's stripes stand out against their background, but the main predators of zebras in most areas where they live are lions. Lions have excellent eyesight, but they are color-blind. They also hunt mainly at night, when the levels of light are very low. For a zebra resting quietly at night, its striped coat provides disruptive camouflage protecting it against lions.

A zebra's stripes can also give a different kind of camouflage. A zebra is well camouflaged when it is seen against a background of other zebras! When zebras are threatened, they gather together in a tight herd that keeps moving. With so many striped bodies packed together, it is hard to pick out one zebra from the rest. The striped patterns hide the shapes of the individual animals.

LOST HERDS

On the Serengeti plains of Africa, wildebeest gather in herds of a million or more. These wildebeest herds are small compared with herds in the past. Just over 100 years ago, 40 million springboks roamed across southern Africa. There were also huge herds of wildebeest and quaggas in the same area.

During the 19th and early 20th centuries, human hunters killed millions of all these species. As a result, springboks now survive mainly in protected areas. The quagga, which looked like a cross between a zebra and a horse, died out altogether.

Individual zebras are hard to pick out from the herd when they are packed together.

Important stripes

A zebra's striped patterns have other functions besides camouflage. Zebras use differences between the striped patterns of different individuals to help recognize each other. There is also a theory that a zebra's striped coat helps protect it from the bites of tsetse flies, blood-sucking insects that carry disease.

Gathering in herds

Herding is an important adaptation for many grazing animals. There is little shelter from predators on the open plains. Grazing animals gather together in large herds to improve their chances of survival. On the Serengeti plains of Africa there may be 200,000 zebras in a herd, or up to 1.3 million wildebeest. When a herd is threatened by predators, the animals gather close together. Animals in the center of the herd are safe from attack. Only slower animals and animals around the edges of the herd are in danger.

25

On the Defensive

Lions are top predators in the areas where they live, and they seem to lead an easy life. However, even lions need to defend themselves from attack. A lion's weapons—its agility, its powerful jaws, and razor-sharp claws—are as important for defense as for catching food.

Surviving childhood

Lion cubs are blind and helpless when they are born. They cannot follow their mother around until they are about three months old. In this early part of their lives, their main defense is to remain still and quiet to avoid predators. If they are disturbed, cubs make explosive spitting noises, but this can only scare off small predators.

By the time they are six or seven months old, lion cubs are eating meat, and by about eleven months they are joining the hunt. Now they must fight to get a share of the kills that the lions make. If prey is scarce, the weakest animals in the pride may starve.

Surviving as adults

As adults, lions have to defend themselves from many attacks. Females with cubs must defend them from predators. Male lions often have to defend themselves from other males. Young males are thrown out of their home pride, and they can only find a new home by taking over a pride from another group of males. They must fight in order to take over a pride, and then they must constantly defend it from other males. Large prey animals, such as buffaloes, are a danger to both male and female lions. Male buffaloes often gather together and charge at lions that come too close to the herd.

In addition to defending themselves from danger, females must also defend their cubs from predators ranging from martial eagles to leopards.

Old enemies

Every time a lion makes a kill, it has to defend the food from others. Other pride members will want their share, but another rival is the spotted hyena. Lion prides are very loose groups and often hunt in small groups or on their own. If a pack of spotted hyenas tracks down two or three female lions at a kill, they will attack and try to drive the lions away. If a male lion is present, hyenas will rarely attack, but then the male will take most of the food.

Hyenas are usually thought of as scavengers, but spotted hyenas are very successful predators. They will steal kills from other animals, even lions.

NO DEFENSE

The only animals that lions cannot defend themselves against are humans. In the 19th century, thousands of lions were killed for sport by big game hunters. Even today there are some people who will pay large amounts of money to hunt and kill lions. Many lions also die in traps set by poachers to catch other animals.

Escaping from Predators

Most mammals are not top predators like lions. They have to defend themselves from many enemies. Different mammal species have adapted in different ways to defend themselves.

Deer have excellent hearing as well as sharp eyesight and a good sense of smell. They can swivel their ears like radar dishes, to find out the direction that a sound is coming from.

Grazing animals

Living in herds helps grazing animals reduce the risk of being attacked by predators (see pages 24 and 25). **Grazing** animals—such as antelopes, zebras, and horses—defend themselves in several other ways. Sharp senses help give early warning of a predator's approach. Grazers have eyes in the sides of their head, which gives them a very wide field of vision. They can spot predators approaching from almost any direction. They also have an excellent sense of smell and of hearing. Living in herds also helps. One animal alone may not notice a predator approaching, but a herd has many eyes, ears, and noses.

Many grazing animals are built for speed and can outrun most predators over long distances. Antelopes and gazelles are also very agile. When impalas run from predators, they take great leaps as they go. These sudden leaps can help them avoid the clutches of a predator.

Some grazers defend themselves by becoming too overpowering to attack. Elephants, rhinos, hippos, and buffaloes are all very large animals with horns or tusks that make them dangerous to attack.

Digging for safety

Small mammals usually keep hidden to avoid their enemies. Most have some kind of camouflage to keep from being seen. Many dig burrows to provide safe places where they can rest and hide from their enemies. In forests they may use holes in trees as dens, or caves in rocky places. Some species, such as gophers and mole rats, dig whole networks of underground tunnels where they spend most of their lives. Burrows usually have several entrances so that, if a predator comes into the burrow one way, the animal can escape through another tunnel. Many burrowing animals feed at night because there are fewer predators by night than by day.

FAST BREEDERS

Despite all their defenses, many small mammals become food for predators. Some mammals have adapted to heavy losses by reproducing quickly. Rabbits, mice, rats, voles, and lemmings are all fast breeders. Mice, for instance, are pregnant for 19 to 21 days and are ready to mate again within 2 days of giving birth. In theory, one pair of mice and their offspring could produce 500 young in just 21 weeks.

Aardvarks have powerful front claws for digging and for breaking open termite mounds. They rest in their burrows by day and go termite hunting at night.

More Defenses

Some mammals have their own unique defenses. Armor, chemicals, sentries, and decoys—you can find all these adaptations in different mammal species.

Armor and chemicals

Hedgehogs, armadillos, and pangolins all protect themselves from predators with armor. Their armored coverings are very different from a mammal's usual fur coat. When they are threatened, they curl up into a ball with no weak spot where a predator can attack. A hedgehog has a covering of strong, sharp spines all across its back and neck. An armadillo has a horny outer shell, while pangolins are covered in hard, pointed scales.

There are two unrelated groups of porcupines—one found in Africa and Asia, the other in the United States. Both have spiny armor like the hedgehog, but the spines are even longer. When threatened, porcupines do not curl up into a ball. Instead, they raise the quills on their back and run backward at their attacker. The predator usually gets a noseful of quills, which break off the porcupine and stay embedded in the muzzle or snout.

Skunks scare off predators with chemicals rather than armor. If threatened, they lift their tails and spray a jet of really stinky, irritating liquid in the face of their attacker. Once an animal has been sprayed in this way, it never attacks a skunk again.

a

These are some unusual mammal defenses:
(a) A skunk spraying.
(b) A pangolin curled into a ball for protection.
(c) A meerkat standing guard.

Sentries and decoys

Some mammals work together to protect themselves from predators. Meerkats live in groups in underground burrows. During the day they feed on insects and any other small animals they can find. While most of the group is feeding, with heads down, one or two meerkats do guard duty. Different meerkats guard each day. The guards do not feed but scan their surroundings watching out for any sign of predators. If they notice anything suspicious, they call out a warning, and all the meerkats run for their burrows.

The coati is a South American relation of the raccoon. When it is threatened the coati has a very unusual way of defending itself. If an enemy gets too close, the coati curls its striped tail over its head and waves it temptingly in front of its face. The predator attacks the waving tail, and the coati attacks the predator's muzzle with its sharp claws.

EXTINCT GIANTS

The biggest living armadillo, the giant armadillo, has a body up to 39 inches (1 meter) long and weighs up to 132 pounds (60 kilograms). This is tiny compared with the size of giant armadillos that lived in the past. Some of these armadillo ancestors were 10 feet (3 meters) long. Native Americans used the shells of these giants as roofs for their tombs.

c

b

Social Cats

Most cats are solitary mammals. They generally live and hunt alone. Lions are different because they live in prides. This improves their survival chances. Lions that live alone do not live as long as lions in prides, and they rarely get the chance to mate.

A loose group

A pride typically has between three and ten adult females and two and four adult males, plus their young. They live together in an area called a territory, where the pride lions do most of their hunting. They will attack and chase away any other lions that come into their territory.

Although there may be up to fourteen adult lions in a pride, they rarely all come together in one place. Smaller groups of lions within the pride hunt or spend time together.

Pride relations

The females in a pride are usually all related. They are often sisters or cousins. The pride males also are often brothers or cousins. However, the males and the females in a pride are not related. The females in the pride often stay with the pride their whole life, but the males are newcomers. They take over the pride by driving out the previous group of pride males.

The lions in a pride do not form lasting pairs. Each male will mate with any or all of the females. Often several females give birth to cubs at about the same time. If this happens, the females raise all the cubs as one group. The females share the job of looking after the cubs, even suckling one another's cubs (feeding them milk). This way of raising young improves the cubs' chances of survival because they are usually never left alone, whereas a single mother must leave her cubs when she goes to hunt.

Lion cubs play and fight together or with adults. Their fights and games are useful training in the skills they will later need for hunting.

Growing up

By the age of eleven months or so, cubs are learning to hunt alongside other pride members. By about two to three years of age, the young females are ready to mate and the young males can hunt for themselves. At this age the males leave the pride. They usually live alone for a couple of years, then look for a pride to take over and make their own.

CUB DEATHS

A group of males can usually only hold onto a pride for two or three years at most. After this a group of younger, stronger males will come along and force out the old group or kill them. When a new group of males takes over, they kill any cubs they find and then mate with the females. However, females sometimes successfully hide or defend their cubs.

Adapting Through Behavior

It usually takes many generations for animals to adapt physically to new environments, but a species can change its behavior much more quickly. More than any other animal group, mammals have been able to adapt their behavior to fit into different habitats.

Sleeping or moving

Many environments are good for part of the year and tough for the rest of the time. Some places have a warm summer and a cold winter, while in other places it is hot and wet for part of the year, then hot and dry for the rest of the time. Some mammals **hibernate** or **aestivate**. Hedgehogs and field mice are among the many mammals in northern Europe that hibernate, while jerboas, ground squirrels, and other small mammals in desert areas aestivate. In hibernation or aestivation, the body shuts down to keep energy use at a minimum.

Other animals survive periods when food is scarce by **migrating,** traveling long distances to places where food is more abundant.

Huge herds of wildebeest and other grazing animals spend the rainy season on the Serengeti plains in Africa. They then move north to the Masai Mara where there is occasional rain, even in the dry season.

Like all rodents, beavers have two chisel-like teeth at the front of their mouth. They can cut down a tree with these teeth.

TAILOR-MADE ENVIRONMENT

Beavers are able to adapt their environment to suit their needs, rather than adapting to fit their environment. First, they dam a river or stream to create a deep lake. Then they build a lodge or den in the middle of the lake they have created. An underwater entrance allows the beavers to get in and out in winter when the lake surface may be iced over.

From solitary to social

Mammals live in all kinds of different societies. At one extreme are mammals that live alone, such as hedgehogs, most cats, and pandas. At the other extreme are mammals that live in huge groups, such as herds of antelopes and zebras, towns of prairie dogs, and huge **maternity colonies** of bats. In between there are mammal groups of all sizes.

Mammals often live alone because food is scarce or hard to get. For instance, it usually takes a polar bear many hours of patient hunting to catch a seal. The help of another bear will not make the seal easier to catch, so polar bears live alone. On the other hand, for caribou feeding in the Arctic in the summer, food is plentiful so there is no harm in sharing it. Also, gathering in herds gives each caribou a better chance of escape from predators.

Finding Mates and Breeding

Reproduction is essential for any species to survive. A species must produce at least enough young to replace the individuals that die. Mammals have evolved in many different ways to make sure that reproduction is a success.

Among African wild dogs both the male and the female help feed the young.

Mammal advantages

Nearly all mammals produce live young. This adaptation has great advantages over laying eggs because the young are protected inside the mother until much later in their development. Suckling their offspring gives mammals another advantage. It means that their young have a guaranteed food supply for the first stage of their life.

FINDING A MATE

Mammals that live in groups can easily find a mate. However, for giant whales living alone, trying to find a mate in the vast ocean can be as hard as trying to find a needle in a haystack. Whales solve this by gathering in a certain part of the ocean during the breeding season. Adult male sperm whales travel north and south to feed in the rich, cold seas of the Arctic and Antarctic. However, female sperm whales and their young spend the year in warm tropical waters. Once each year male sperm whales travel to the tropics to find a mate.

Bigger is better

In many mammals, especially in larger species, the male is bigger and stronger than the female. Male lions, for example, are more than 20 percent bigger than lionesses.

In many mammal societies, males mate with more than one female and have little or nothing to do with raising the young. However, in some groups, such as the dog family, the male mates with only one female and helps feed the young. With two parents feeding them, the young get more food. This allows them to grow more quickly, which may give them a better chance of survival.

Male sperm whales do not breed until they are nearly 30 years old. Then they travel from the polar seas to the tropics to find females in the oceans close to the Equator.

Faster or slower

Producing an animal the size of a shrew uses far less energy than producing an elephant. For this reason, small mammals generally reproduce faster than larger mammals. A lemming, for instance, can produce up to 12 babies when it is only 42 days old, whereas an elephant cannot breed until it is at least 10 years old and then takes 22 months to produce a single calf.

Failing to Adapt

Modern lions first appeared only about 750,000 years ago, but similar mammal species have been around for millions of years. Mammals have successfully adapted and changed to fit in with their environment since they first appeared nearly 200 million years ago. However, human activities are changing the world so fast that animals cannot adapt quickly enough to the changes. Nearly 25 percent of all mammal species are now in danger of extinction.

The coastal temperate rainforests of the western United States and Canada are rich in wildlife. However, half of this hillside has been clear-cut, destroying the habitat of many animals.

Nowhere to live

As the human population grows and grows, people take over grasslands, cut down forests, and drain wetlands to make space for farmland and cities. As people use up more and more space, there is less space left for wild animals. This habitat loss is the main cause of the decline in mammal numbers.

Large predators, such as lions and other big cats, are especially at risk from habitat loss. They need an area with enough prey animals to keep them alive. In habitats rich with prey, this could be as small as 7.7 square miles (20 square kilometers) but in an area poor in prey it could be over 154.4 square miles (400 square kilometers). Outside of game reserves and national parks, there are very few areas of wild land big enough to support lions and other large carnivores.

SUCCESS STORIES?

Although most mammal species are declining, a few species have learned to live around humans and are increasing in numbers. The roof rat, house mouse, and Norway rat all originally lived in Central Asia and India, but they are now found around the world. The numbers of rats and mice are now so great that they are pests, spoiling food and spreading diseases.

On the edge

Lions as a group are not yet in danger of becoming extinct. However, other large cats are at risk of dying out completely. Tiger populations dropped from 100,000 to about 7,500 in the 20th century, and several tiger subspecies have died out. Snow leopards are among the most endangered of all cats. Numbers are very low and because they live in remote mountains, it is hard to figure out how many snow leopards remain in the wild.

Carnivores are not the only mammals at risk. On the island of Madagascar, over 90 percent of the rainforest has been cut for timber, and all species of **lemur** on the island are endangered.

Orangutans and giant pandas are two other species that are close to extinction because their forest habitat is small and fragile.

Although hunting wild tigers is illegal, many are still killed for their fur and bones, which are used in traditional medicine in some countries. These skins were found near Delhi, India.

39

Unfair Competition

Competition between species is an important part of how animals adapt to their environment. In the past 200 years or so, humans have changed the rules of the competition by bringing species from one part of the world to another. In a new environment, animals have no natural predators, so their numbers grow. Sometimes the animals have been moved from one place to another accidentally. Rats have spread across the world by riding in cargo ships, but some species have been introduced on purpose.

Red squirrels are found on the Isle of Wight and a few areas in southern England. They are also still seen in the forests of northern England and in Scotland, but the gray squirrel is seen almost everywhere in the United Kingdom.

Gray terror

In 1876 T. V. Brocklehurst released a pair of gray squirrels from the United States into the grounds of his home in Cheshire, England, in the United Kingdom. At around the same time, other gray squirrels also were released in other parts of the United Kingdom. The gray squirrels thrived and quickly spread. Two squirrels released in Scotland, for instance, produced many offspring, and 25 years later the squirrels had spread over an area of 300 square miles (777 square kilometers).

The gray squirrel was in direct competition with the European red squirrel. The red squirrel is about half the size of the gray squirrel and cannot feed on such a wide variety of foods. Gray squirrels are also more resistant to disease than red squirrels. In most areas, the red squirrel was wiped out and is now found only in a few small areas of the United Kingdom.

In 1948 gray squirrels were released in Italy. They now have spread over much of Italy, and there are fears that they soon will spread to the rest of Europe and wipe out the red squirrel altogether.

Bunny terror

In 1859 Thomas Austin brought 24 rabbits over from the United Kingdom and released them on his estate in Victoria, Australia. He wanted a few rabbits to hunt for sport, but he got more than he bargained for. Rabbits breed very quickly, and within a short time the original 24 rabbits had become many thousands more. They spread quickly across the country, causing all kinds of damage. Within ten years Australians were killing two million rabbits a year and still not reducing their numbers. Farmers and governments built thousands of miles of fences to try to keep rabbits out of other parts of the country, but without success. Today, rabbits have spread to nearly all parts of Australia.

Rabbits are placental mammals, but all the native mammals of Australia are marsupials. Ten percent of marsupial species in Australia are now extinct and nearly 25 percent are threatened.

This fence in Queensland, Australia, was built to keep rabbits from crossing the countryside. However, they have not been very successful.

DAMAGE FROM RABBITS

Rabbits in Australia have had many more effects besides out-competing other mammals. They are a terrible pest on farmland, causing millions of dollars of damage to crops each year. The rabbits also have had an effect on the land itself. Their burrows weaken the ground, which collapses during heavy rains, causing widespread **erosion**.

What Makes an Animal Successful?

Lions and other mammals have adapted to life in their particular habitats, both through changes in their bodies and changes in their behavior. Habitats are always changing, and animals have to adapt as their environment changes. If they do not adapt, they die out.

The changes that humans have made to natural habitats over the last few hundred years have been very rapid. Few animals can adapt to the complete destruction of their environment. These changes have been most damaging to large animals, which need more space, and to animals that have become specialized to a particular lifestyle.

Lemurs are specialized for forest life, but most of their habitat has been destroyed. They have not been able to adapt to live in non-forest areas, so most lemurs are now endangered.

Lions lose out

Lions and other big cats are both large and specialized. They have been hunted out of most places where they used to live because they threaten humans and their livestock. Animals such as leopards and tigers have also been hunted for their fur.

Big cats are specialized to prey on large animals. They are very good at this, but they need large numbers of prey animals to survive. Small areas of protected land are not good for big cats because they cannot support enough prey animals for the cats to feed on.

Generalists do better

Animals that are generalists are better able to adapt when habitats change. They are not well-adapted to one habitat, but are skilled at surviving in many different places. Animals from the dog family—such as wolves, foxes, and coyotes—are less fussy than big cats about what they eat. They will eat fruit, scraps, and even worms if nothing else is available. Foxes and coyotes have managed to adapt to live alongside humans, despite being heavily hunted. However, wolves are too large for humans to live comfortably alongside, and their numbers have fallen drastically.

Foxes are generalists that can adapt to a wide range of different habitats. They have learned to live with people in the hearts of cities. This fox is outside 10 Downing Street, home of the prime minister of the United Kingdom.

WOLF SUCCESS

Gray wolves used to be common across the United States, but by the mid-20th century they were endangered or threatened in all states except Alaska. In 1995 wolves were reintroduced in three areas, one of which was Yellowstone National Park. All three wolf populations have survived and flourished.

Can humans adapt?

Humans are generalists, like foxes, rats, and mice. We manage to live in almost all habitats on Earth. People are found in the frozen wastes of the Arctic and in the heat of the desert. Humans thrive in tropical jungles and on mountain slopes. However, people tend to adapt to different habitats by changing the environment rather than by adapting their behavior to fit the environment. If humans can adapt to live alongside other mammals, rather than getting rid of them, the rich variety of life today will survive. If humans continue to destroy the things that other mammals need to live, however, only a few mammal species will survive.

43

Further Information

Lion facts

Scientific name:	Panthera leo
Size (head and body):	Male: 8.5–10.8 ft. (1.7–2.5 m)
	Female: 5.2–6.2 ft. (1.6–1.9 m)
Feeding mode	Predator
Habitat	Savannah, grassland, open woodlands, semi-desert
Camouflage	Good; blends in with environment
Distribution	Africa from south Sahara to southern Africa; Gujerat, India

Mammal record-breakers

Largest ever mammal	Blue whale	Length: 109 ft. 4 in. (33.27 m) Weight: 157 tons
Largest ever land mammal	Rhinoceros	Weight: 14.7–19.7 tons
Largest land mammal	African elephant	Height: 10 ft 6 in. (3.2 m) Weight: 5.9 tons
Smallest land mammal	Savi's pigmy shrew or	Length: 1.4 in. (36 mm) Weight: 0.04 oz. (1.2 g)
	Kitti's hog-nosed bat (bumblebee bat)	Length: 1.2 in. (31 mm) Weight: 0.07 oz. (2.0 g)
Fastest mammal	Cheetah	71 mph. (114 km/h)
Slowest mammal	Three-toed sloth	0.07–0.1mph (0.11–0.16 km/h), meaning it would take 14 hours to travel 1 mile
Fattest mammal	Ringed seal pup	50% of body weight is fat at **weaning**
Tallest mammal	Giraffe	Tallest recorded was a male 19 ft. (5.8 m) tall
Biggest land predator	Siberian tiger	Length: 10 ft. (3.1 m) Weight: 569 lb. (258 kg)
Biggest sea predator	Sperm whale	Length: 52 ft 6 in. (16 m) Weight: 56 tons

Longest migration	Gray whale	Round trip of about 12,000 miles (19,300 km) each year, from Baja California to coast of Alaska and back
Smelliest	Skunk	Spray can be smelled at concentration of 10 part per billion (1 teaspoonful in an Olympic-size swimming pool)
Largest herds of hoofed mammals	Springboks	In the early 20th century, herds of 10 million animals were seen. Herds were 15 miles (25 km) wide and 100 miles (160 km) long.

Books

- *DK Eyewitness: Mammal.* New York: DK Children, 2004.
  – Informative book packed with information and photographs of mammals
- Feeney, Kathy. *Our Wild World: Leopards.* Minnetonka, Minn.: Northword Press, 2002.
  – Information, facts, and photos introduce readers to the leopard
- Winner, Cherie. *Our Wild World: Lions.* Minnetonka, Minn.: Northword Press, 2001.
  – Lots of information about how lions live, sleep, eat, and raise their young

Websites

- The cat specialist group of the World Conservation Union
  www.catsg.org
  – Information on all 36 wild cat species, written by leading cat scientists

- Yahooligans: Mammals
  yahooligans.yahoo.com/content/animals/mammals/
  – Short but informative pages on a large number of different mammals

- Zoom Mammals
  www.enchantedlearning.com/subjects/mammals/
  – A simple but informative website on all kinds of mammals

Glossary

absorb take in or soak up, like a sponge

adaptation change that helps a living thing fit into its environment

adapted when a living thing has changed to fit in with its environment

aestivate sleep through the dry season

carnassial scissor-like cheek tooth designed for slicing flesh

camouflage coloring and patterning that help an animal hide from its enemies or blend into its environment

canine tooth dagger-like front tooth

carcass dead body of an animal

carnivore meat-eating animal

cell tiny building block of all living things

compete fight with another animal for food, shelter, or a mate

countershading coloring that makes an animal's body look flat and less visible

direct competition when two species of living things live in the same habitat and eat the same foods. Eventually one species will become dominant and the other will become extinct.

disruptive camouflage markings that break up an animal's outline and make it harder to see

erosion removal of pieces of rock or soil that have been worn away by the weather

evolution process by which life on Earth has developed and changed

extinct when all animals of a certain species die out

filter feeder living thing that gets food by straining small creatures or tiny pieces of food from water

gamete male or female sex cell, usually sperm or egg

gene something that is transferred from a parent to its offspring that determines some features of that offspring

generalist living thing that can live in a variety of habitats

grazing eating grass

habitat place where an animal lives

herbivore animal that feeds on plants

hibernate sleep through the winter

insectivore insect-eating animal

lemur one of 50 forest-dwelling primates found only in Madagascar

mammal warm-blooded, usually furry animal that feeds its young on milk

mammary gland organ that gives milk

marsupial mammal, such as a kangaroo or a wombat, that gives birth to a very undeveloped baby and then looks after it in a pouch on its belly

mate animal's breeding partner; also when a male and female animal come together to produce young

maternity colony large gathering of female bats or other animals that get together to give birth and look after their young

meteorite rock that falls from space and hits Earth's surface

migrate travel long distances each year from a summer breeding area to a winter feeding ground

natural selection mechanism of evolution by which only those individuals that are best fitted to their habitat and lifestyle survive and reproduce

niche particular place and way of life of one individual species within a habitat

offspring young of an animal

omnivore animal that eats both animal and plant food

placental mammal mammal that has a longer pregnancy than a marsupial and gives birth to better-developed young

predator animal that hunts and kills other animals for food

prey animal that is eaten by a predator

pride group of lions

range places where a living thing is known to live

reproduce produce young

ruminant mammal whose digestive system is specialized to eat plants and who chews its food several times before it is digested

savannah area of mixed grassland and thorny trees

scavenger animal that eats scraps, dead and rotten meat, or any food available

species group of very similar animals that can breed together to produce healthy young

territory area that animals defend against other animals of the same species

top predator predator at the top of the food chain that is not the prey of another animal

variation difference among individuals within a species

vertebrate animal with a backbone, such as mammals, birds, reptiles, and amphibians

warm-blooded able to keep the body at a constant temperature

weaning process of introducing a young mammal to food other than its mother's milk

INDEX